KU-737-068

Everything you need to know about
FROGS

AND OTHER SLIPPERY CREATURES

DK

LONDON, NEW YORK, MUNICH,
MELBOURNE, and DELHI

Senior editor Carrie Love
Senior designer Claire Patané
Design Hedi Hunter and Rosie Levine
Editorial Holly Beaumont, Fleur Star,
Ben Morgan, and Alexander Cox

Consultant Brian Groombridge

Publishing manager Bridget Giles
Art director Martin Wilson
Creative director Jane Bull
Category publisher Mary Ling
Production editor Clare McLean
Production controller Claire Pearson
Picture researcher Rob Nunn
Proofreaders Caroline Stamps and
Lorrie Mack
Jacket editor Matilda Gollon

First published in Great Britain in 2011
by Dorling Kindersley Limited
80 Strand, London WC2R 0RL
Penguin Group (UK)

10 9 8 7 6 5 4 3 2 1
001–179459–Aug/11

Copyright © 2011 Dorling Kindersley Limited

All rights reserved. No part of this publication
may be reproduced, stored in a retrieval system,
or transmitted in any form or by any means,
electronic, mechanical, photocopying,
recording, or otherwise, without the prior
written permission of the copyright owner.

A CIP catalogue record for this book
is available from the British Library.

ISBN: 978-1-4053-6836-0

Printed and bound in China by Hung Hing

**Discover more at
www.dk.com**

Can you
SEE ME?
**This high-casqued
chameleon** (*Chamaeleo
hoehnelii*) is superb at blending in
with its surroundings. Find out
more about camouflage
on page 17.

CONTENTS

How does a fer-de-lance snake kill its prey? Discover its tactic on **page 39**.

Ribbit,

scuttle,

Which lizard is an insectivore? Take a look at **page 46**.

Why is the male midwife toad a hands-on father? See for yourself on **page 25**.

How can you survive an attack from a crocodile or alligator? Read and REMEMBER the tips on **page 71**.

How far can a leatherback sea turtle travel? Take a journey with one on **pages 60–61**.

Try to outstare a frog on **pages 30–31**. One frog will always win as it has a spot that looks like an eye!

How does a reptile obtain heat from its surroundings? Get a glimpse on **page 28**.

slither

Play a game of snakes and ladders on **pages 50–51**. Be careful or you might slip down an inland taipan!

When a frog sheds its skin what does it do with it? Discover the answer on **page 13**.

Amphibians

Amphibians are animals that live PARTLY in *water* and PARTLY on land. **Frogs**, toads, NEWTS, and salamanders are all **amphibians**.

REPTILES have dry, *scaly skin,* but AMPHIBIANS have **soft**, moist skin. Most amphibians can breathe **through their skin**, but only if it stays *damp*. Adult amphibians can also BREATHE through lungs.

HOW MANY?

There are about **6,800** species of amphibians, most of which are *frogs*. There are about **600** species of newt and *salamander*.

Frog spawn

Most *amphibians* breed in **water**. Unlike reptiles, which lay **tough-shelled eggs** on **land**, most amphibians lay *soft, jelly-like eggs* in **water**.

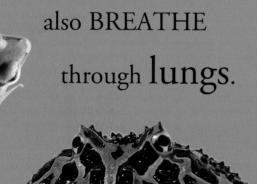

Is a toad a frog?

I have dry, lumpy skin that looks like it's covered in warts. People usually call me a toad, but I'm really a frog.

I'm a tree frog

Most frogs live near a **river or pools of water**. But in *rainforests it is so humid*, the trees are **wet** all the time allowing some frogs to stay in them permanently. They are called *tree frogs* and have **huge, sticky fingers** to help them climb.

Most baby amphibians live entirely in **water.** Called **tadpoles**, they **swim like fish** and *breathe through gills.* As they grow up, they develop legs and crawl onto land, but they must always be in wet places.

Tadpoles

When a **tadpole** hatches out of an egg, its first task in life is to *eat what's left of its egg*, which is **full of nutrients**. In most amphibians, the tadpole changes into an adult by a process called **metamorphosis**.

Reptiles

Today there are more than **9,000 reptile** *species* on Earth; the major groups are **alligators** and *crocodiles*, TURTLES, **lizards**, and *snakes*. ALL REPTILES are **cold-blooded**, which is why they WARM THEMSELVES in *the sun*, and have bodies covered in **dry**, HORNY SCALES. Some reptiles lay eggs; others give birth to live young.

8

HOW MANY?

Lizards make up the largest group of reptiles (with 5,461 species), followed by snakes (3,315 species), then turtles (317 species). There are fewer amphisbaenians (181 species), and even fewer crocodilians (24 species). The smallest group are the tuataras (with just 2 species).

Brightly coloured

Iguanas and their relatives make up some of the most colourful of all lizards. This Green iguana is brightly coloured with a few markings.

All reptiles have backbones

Bright lines

The red markings on a Madagascan giant day gecko vary between individuals.

Reptiles vary greatly in *shape* and *size*. However, *all reptiles* have **scales** in contrast to the **smooth**, moist skin of amphibians. Scales differ amongst species, but they are a defining *feature* of a reptile.

Legless and long

Snakes are legless reptiles. They're found all over the world, but they don't do well in cold places. The Common boa constrictor, such as the one shown here, can grow to 1–4 m (3–13ft)!

Light like sand

Like many geckos, this Sandstone gecko is coloured to blend in with its surroundings.

Tuataras are a group of **reptiles,** found only in **New Zealand.**

What's inside?

FROGS **have simple skeletons** with fewer bones than other *vertebrates* (animals with backbones). They tend to have a robust body and strong hind limbs. Most frogs have protruding eyes and no tail. Take a look at what's under a frog's skin.

Skull

Frogs tend to have a broad head with large sockets for the eyes. They usually have a short spine and no ribs.

The hands and fingers of frogs vary according to lifestyle. Climbing frogs need fingers that can grip well.

Hand

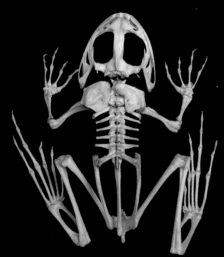

Heart **CHAMBERS**

Frogs have a developed nervous system that is made up of a brain, nerves, and spinal cord. A frog's heart has three chambers, whereas mammals have four.

A frog's brain has similar structures to a human's brain. The cerebellum (region on the top of the brain) controls posture and muscular coordination.

Elongated ankle bones

Toe bone

A frog's bone structue helps it jump a long way. The *tibia* (shinbone) and *fibula* (calf bone) are fused into a single, strong bone.

The legs and feet of frogs vary depending on where they live. Frogs that live in water have webbed toes. The more time spent in water, the more webbed their toes are.

SNAKES have an incredibly LONG neck. It takes up one third of their length. Their **organs** are also ong and fit in *one behind the other.*

Their heart is encased in a sac, but it's not fixed in place, preventing damage from swallowing a large animal.

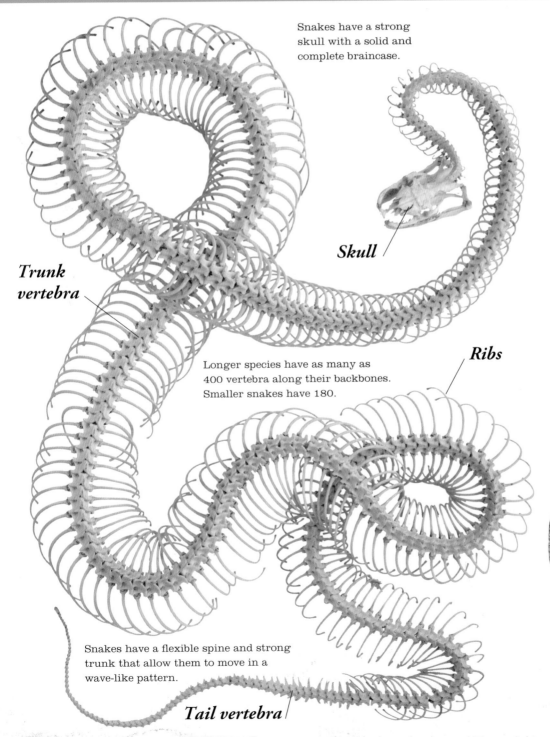

Snakes have a strong skull with a solid and complete braincase.

Skull

Trunk vertebra

Longer species have as many as 400 vertebra along their backbones. Smaller snakes have 180.

Ribs

Snakes have a flexible spine and strong trunk that allow them to move in a wave-like pattern.

Tail vertebra

Dry SKIN

Snakes have dry, smooth skin that is covered in scales. They shed their skin regularly. When they shed their skin it comes off as a whole layer and is often intact.

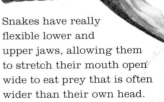

Snakes have really flexible lower and upper jaws, allowing them to stretch their mouth open wide to eat prey that is often wider than their own head.

SUPER

Frogs have very **special skin.** *They don't just*

FROGS don't usually SWALLOW *water like we do.*

Instead, they absorb most of the **moisture** they need

through *their skin.* They also get water

from prey that they eat. Their skin is used to get **extra**

oxygen from the water (in addition to the oxygen

that's come into their lungs via their mouth cavity).

Because frogs only get oxygen through their skin

when it's moist, they need to take good care of it or

they might suffocate. Some frogs are **slimy.** This is

because their SKIN secretes a

mucus that stops it from getting dry.

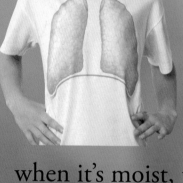

SKIN

wear it, they also **drink** and **breathe** through it!

Frogs regularly shed their outermost layer of skin cells to keep it healthy. This looks **pretty yucky.** They start to *twist and turn* and act like they have the **hiccups.** They do this to *stretch* out of their old skin! Finally, they pull the skin OFF over their head LIKE A SWEATER, and then *(this is gross)* they EAT IT! **Eeeeewww!**

Life cycle of a frog

From a baby tadpole to a young frog

Life begins

A male and a female frog come together to **mate**. Eggs are laid in *clumps* or strings. An egg *hatches* about **six days** after it's been fertilised. At first it feeds on the remains of the yolk.

Tiny tadpoles

When an egg hatches, a **tadpole's** mouth, tail, and external gills are not fully developed. At about **seven to ten days**, a tadpole begins to **feed on algae** and attaches itself to weeds.

Fully formed

Between **12 to 16 weeks** a frog has completed its *growth cycle.* The timing varies between species and on the food and water supply. A fully formed frog starts the process afresh by mating.

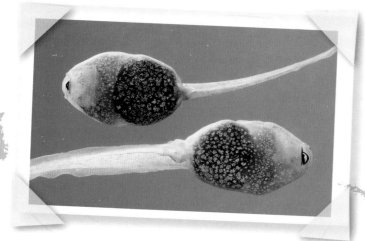

Getting bigger

At **four weeks** the *external gills* are covered by body skin. They eventually disappear and are replaced with lungs. Tadpoles have *tiny teeth* that help them to chew away at plants and algae-covered surfaces.

A bit of both

Tiny legs start to form from **six to nine weeks**. The head becomes more obvious. The *arms begin to come out*, with the elbows showing first. After **nine weeks** the tadpole is beginning to look more like a frog.

Nearly there!

By **12 weeks** the young froglet only has a small stub of a *tail*. It looks like a smaller version of an adult frog. Soon it will leave the water to live on the ground.

15

COLOURS and
MARKINGS

AMPHIBIANS and REPTILES have a variety of *markings* and **colours.** The spectrum ranges from bright reds and blues to muddy *greens* and BROWNS. Some have **spots** while others have *stripes.*

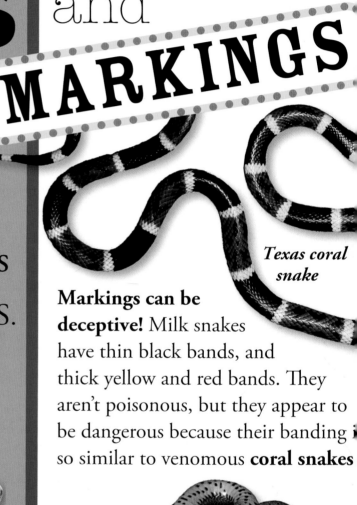

Texas coral snake

Markings can be deceptive! Milk snakes have thin black bands, and thick yellow and red bands. They aren't poisonous, but they appear to be dangerous because their banding is so similar to venomous **coral snakes**.

Regal ring-neck snake

Fire salamander

Red-eyed tree frog

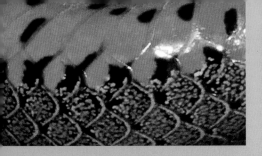

Southern dwarf chameleon

Colourful CAMOUFLAGE

The pattern and colour of an amphibian or reptile can help them to blend in with their surroundings to hide from predators. Chameleons, as their name suggests, have an amazing ability to hide themselves by changing their appearance. They can alter their colour as well as their markings.

Strawberry poison-dart frogs are bright red. This acts to warn other creatures that their skin secretions are highly toxic.

Collared lizard

Hide and seek

The Pacific tree frog is able to blend into its surroundings very easily. It reacts to seasonal changes and can switch its colouring from brown to green. It can also change its markings and the lightness of its skin according to the shift in background brightness.

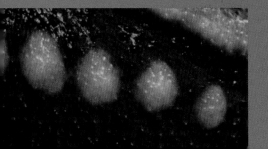

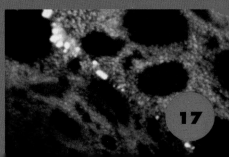

Home, Sweet Home

Amphibians are found on all continents except Antarctica. Nearly all amphibians live in or near wet areas such as streams, rivers, ponds, lakes, and other wetlands, but some display amazing adaptations that allow them to live in dry, dusty deserts. Many adult amphibians spend their lives on land, but nearly all need to lay their eggs in water.

Desert **LIVING**

The **desert tortoise** (*Gopherus agassizii*) spends about 95 per cent of its life under ground. It can go a year without water.

Couch's spadefoot toad (*Scaphiophus couchii*) gets its name from its feet, which help it to dig down through loose sand. It lives underground during dry months.

The **sandfish** (*Scincus scincus*) lives in Africa's Sahara desert and is famous for its ability to "swim" through sand.

Plant **LIFE**

The female **strawberry poison-dart frog** (*Oophaga pumilio*) lays her eggs on a leaf. When the tadpoles hatch, she moves them to a water-filled location.

The **gold frog** (*Brachycephalus didactylus*) makes its home in mountain rainforests. It mainly lives among leaf litter. It is a ground-dweller as it can't jump or climb very well. The female lays eggs that hatch directly into small frogs, missing out the tadpole stage.

Up in the **TREES**

The **red-eyed tree frog** (*Agalychnis callidryas*) lives high up in rainforest canopies in Central America. It is also known as the "monkey frog" because of its excellent climbing skills.

The **tree hole frog** (*Metaphryne sundana*) is a native of lowland forests in Borneo. It lives in the hollows of tree trunks. The little frog uses tree hollows to amplify its mating calls so that it can be heard over long distances.

Who lives in a dry place? Many reptiles live in deserts. They can hide from the extreme temperatures in burrows. The desert is the last place you might expect to find an amphibian but a few species have adapted to

Who lives in a house like this? Some frogs have adapted to live in dead leaves that have fallen onto the forest floor whereas others cleverly use leaves to hide their eggs in until they hatch.

Who lives up in the trees? Most of the world's frogs live in tropical rainforests, where the temperature is nice and high and there is plenty of water.

Reptiles don't exist in Antarctica either. Unlike amphibians, they have a watertight skin. This means that they don't dry as quickly. Some reptiles live in hot, dry places such as deserts. Others live in warm swamps, rivers, or forests. A few have even adapted to a life at sea, but all return to land to lay their eggs.

All at **SEA**

In the **WET**

Cool **CREATURES**

The **yellow-bellied sea snake** *(Pelamis platurus)* has the largest lung of any snake. This helps it to control bouyancy so it can stay under water for long periods of time (up to three and a half hours).

The **African clawed frog** *(Xenopus laevis)* lives in ponds, lakes, or streams in southern Africa. It spends most of its time in water.

The **wood frog** *(Rana sylvatica)* survives freezing conditions by hibernating. It finds cracks in rocks, or gaps in logs, or can bury itself in leaves, to get through the cold winters.

The **hawksbill turtle** *(Eretmochelys imbricata)* uses its narrow beak to forage for molluscs, sponges, and other animals.

Northern water snake *(Nerodia sipedon)* lives in and around streams, ponds, lakes, and marshes. Water snakes are good swimmers. They have been known to herd tadpoles to the water's edge before tucking in.

Slow worm *(Anguis fragilis)* is a legless lizard that hibernates in piles of leaves, or in hollows between tree roots. It goes to sleep in October and emerges in March to breed in early summer.

Who's that in the sea? Amphibians can't cope with seawater because their skin is too thin to protect them from all the salt. Reptiles have thicker skin and a few species can regulate the salt in their blood and are therefore able to

Who likes to live somewhere moist? Amphibians provide tasty meals for many reptiles, so where they live you will often find reptiles too. The Northern water snake lives near ponds where it can catch amphibians

Who's hiding from the cold? Some reptiles and amphibians live in temperate parts of the world, with cold winters. One of the ways in which they can survive these cold months is to save energy by hibernating.

Amazon horned FROG

Famed for its big appetite and its bad temper, the Amazon horned frog can grow to reach the size of a small dinner plate.

ENORMOUS GAPE
With a mouth that is wider than the length of its body, the Amazon horned frog can gobble up prey almost as big as itself.

Patient **PREDATOR**

Amazon horned frogs are voracious carnivores. They ambush their prey by sitting quietly and waiting for it to approach, before striking with a sudden snap of their jaws. **Amazon horned frogs aren't picky eaters.** Mostly they live on a diet of ants and other insects, but they will try to eat any animal smaller than themselves including mice and, occasionally, rats. They don't always get it right, and may try to take on an animal that is too big for them to stomach.

Watch your feet! The Amazon horned frog will sometimes defend itself by attacking people if it is disturbed. They tend to grab anything that comes near them that could be edible.

Impressive **HORNS**

As its name suggests, the Amazon horned frog has big fleshy horns above its eyes. These are the largest horns of any of the horned frog species. These pointed brows help to disguise the frog's shape as it sits amongst the leaves on the forest floor awaiting its prey.

• Unlike other tadpoles, Amazon horned frog tadpoles are **predatory** from the start. When they hatch they attack other tadpoles and even attack each other.
• Females lay up to **1,000** eggs! They lay their eggs around aquatic plants.
• Males are **slightly smaller** than females. They make a mating call that sounds like a cow lowing (making a "moo" sound).

This frog grows up to 20 cm (8 in) in length.

How do **crocodiles** breathe **underwater** ?

Crocodiles have an amazing ability to breathe and hunt underwater at the same time. By closing a flap of skin at the back of their throat they prevent any water flowing into their lungs. They hold air in their lungs until they resurface. They are able to keep their mouth open to grab prey underwater, although they usually move to land to swallow it. **They also have flaps that can be closed over the nostril and ear openings.**

Saltwater crocodile *(Crocodylus porosus)*

TURTLES
Aquatic turtles breathe through their lungs. The Florida softshell (right) has to surface and use its snout to fill its lungs with oxygen above water. Some turtles manage to stay under water for weeks, living on very low oxygen levels.

Florida softshell turtle *(Apalone ferox)*

Crocodiles can **waterproof their eyes** with a

FROGS

Frogs can breathe through their skin when they're under water. Their skin absorbs oxygen from the water around them. Find out more about their amazing skin on pages 12–13.

Okinawa frog
(Rana sp.)

SEA SNAKES

Sea snakes can stay under water for up to five hours. They have an enlarged lung which helps them to store lots of oxygen for when they're underwater. They have to resurface to breathe in more oxygen before they can make another dive.

Banded sea snake
(Laticauda colubrina)

CROCODILIANS have a FLAP of tissue behind the **tongue** *that covers* their **throats** when they are *submerged* in WATER.

membrane that acts as a **transparent shield**.

AMPHIBIANS and REPTILES have **different** ways of *bringing their young* into the world. Most reptiles and amphibians **hatch from an egg.**

Amphibian eggs

A lot of amphibians lay their eggs in water, where they develop into tiny tadpoles.

However, many amphibians choose a sheltered egg-laying location where they guard their eggs or protect them in a layer of foam.

Other amphibians carry eggs on their back, in their vocal sac, in a skin pocket, or even in their stomach!

Reptile eggs

Most lizards lay eggs. They rarely return to their nests, although some skinks stay with their eggs to help maintain moisture and warmth.

Alligators and caimans make their nests from mounds of soil and leaves. Crocodiles and gavials lay their eggs in holes they dig in sand or dry, crumbly soil.

The shells of eggs laid by most turtles and tortoises are hard, but the shells of marine and river turtle eggs are softer.

However, some FROGS, SNAKES, and LIZARDS give birth to **live young**. There are various parenting styles amongst reptiles and amphibians.

Father **FIGURES**

In some species of frog, the father plays a key role. The male Darwin's frog takes care of the eggs as they develop. When the tadpoles hatch he puts them in his vocal sac, where they grow, until they are released as tiny frogs.

The male midwife toad (right) shows an interesting form of care. The female lays the eggs, but the male carries them on his legs! After about three weeks, the male takes the eggs to water, where the tadpoles hatch.

Absent **PARENTS**

The majority of geckos lay their eggs in bark or in crevices of rocks. Geckos DO NOT take care of their young. The young are self sufficient from birth. Turtles lay the most eggs out of all reptiles, but they don't watch over them. The eggs are left in earth or sand and when the baby turtles emerge, they are on their own. They have to learn survival skills pretty quickly!

When a caiman or alligator is born, it stays close to its mother. The young reptiles are protected by their mother in the early weeks of their life. When danger is detected they can use their mother as a shield by hiding under her body.

Boy or girl? The gender of baby crocodiles, turtles, and tortoises is often decided by the temperature during incubation.

ACTUAL SIZE

from this.................................*to this!*

The GOLIATH FROG starts out SMALL. Its tadpole is the same size as that of the average frog, but it **keeps on growing** until it reaches the *size of a cat.* With legs outstretched, the *frog* can MEASURE almost 1 m (3 ft) in length.

The goliath frog
(*Conraua goliath*)
lives in western Africa. It is found across a narrow range of Equatorial Guinea and Cameroon, in and around fast-flowing rivers and waterfalls. It is a popular food for locals.

Goliath frog
The goliath frog is the largest anuran (the class of animals that includes frogs and toads).

How small?
The smallest frog in the world is the Monte Iberia frog (*Eleutherodactylus iberia*) of Cuba. This tiny amphibian reaches a full size of only 9.8 mm (0.38 in) from snout to vent. It would sit comfortably on one of your fingernails.

Smallest frog
The Monte Iberia frog breeds by direct development, missing out the tadpole stage altogether.

SUN seekers

**Reptiles
are cold-blooded animals,**
although once they have *sunbathed* their
blood is about the same temperature as ours.
Most reptiles live in **warm climates** as
they rely on their surroundings
to obtain heat.

Reptiles keep their
internal temperature at a
constant level by moving to
and from the shade.

A reptile can also obtain heat
by resting its belly on a
warm rock.

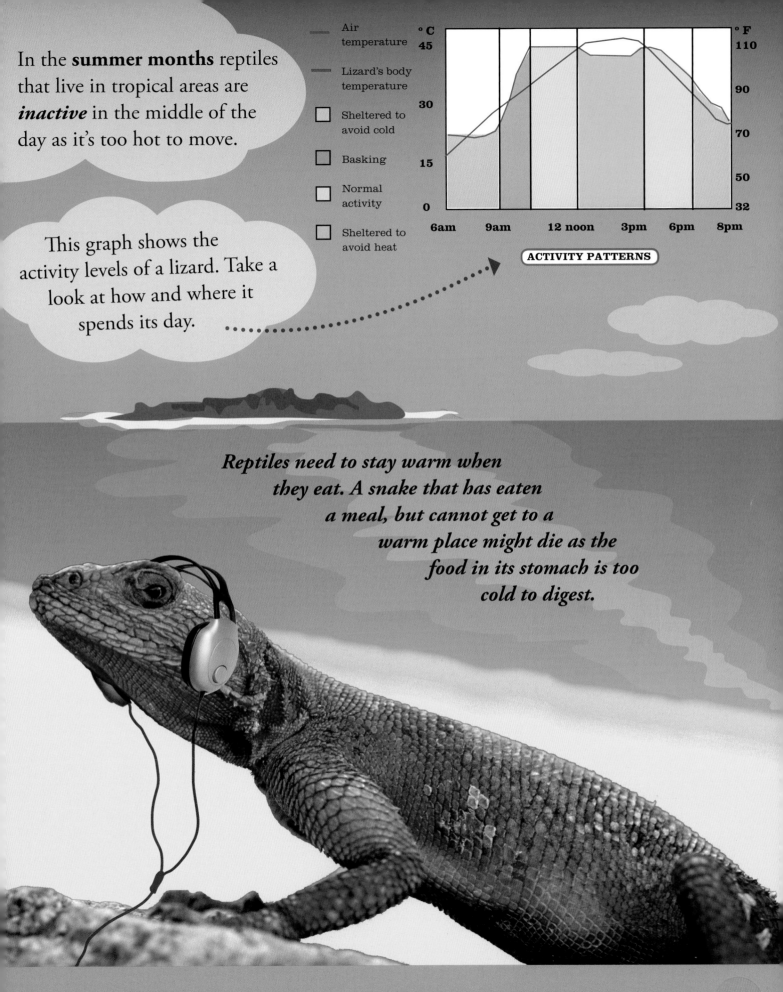

In the **summer months** reptiles that live in tropical areas are *inactive* in the middle of the day as it's too hot to move.

This graph shows the activity levels of a lizard. Take a look at how and where it spends its day.

Air temperature

Lizard's body temperature

☐ Sheltered to avoid cold

☐ Basking

☐ Normal activity

☐ Sheltered to avoid heat

°C
45
30
15
0

°F
110
90
70
50
32

6am   9am   12 noon   3pm   6pm   8pm

ACTIVITY PATTERNS

Reptiles need to stay warm when they eat. A snake that has eaten a meal, but cannot get to a warm place might die as the food in its stomach is too cold to digest.

species will hibernate until the temperature is right. 29

Can you spot the FAKE?

FROGS use their MARKINGS for protection against *predators.* One of the frogs shown here has a cleverly positioned eyespot that *helps* it to confuse any potential ATTACKERS. Can you tell which one it is?

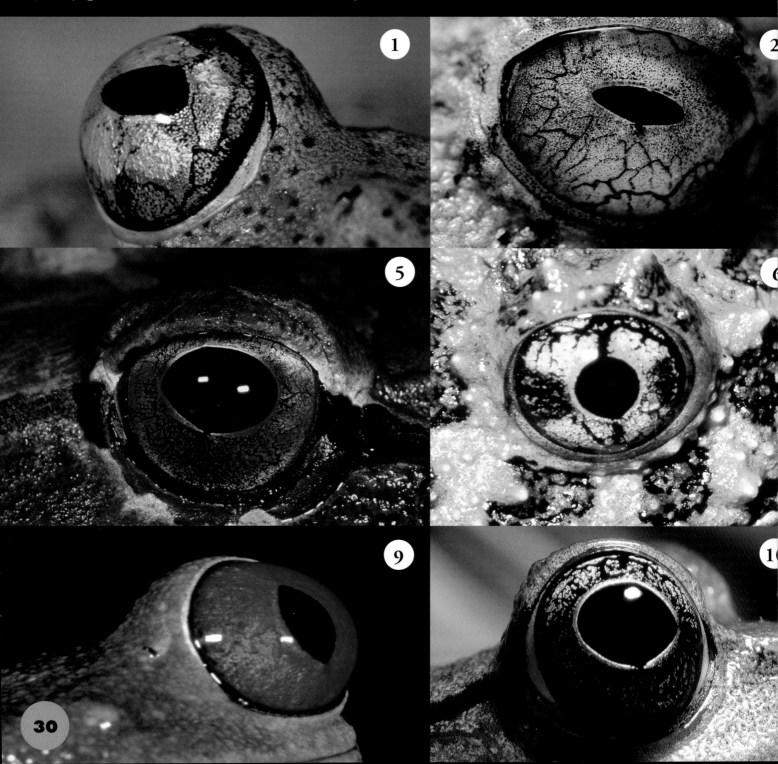

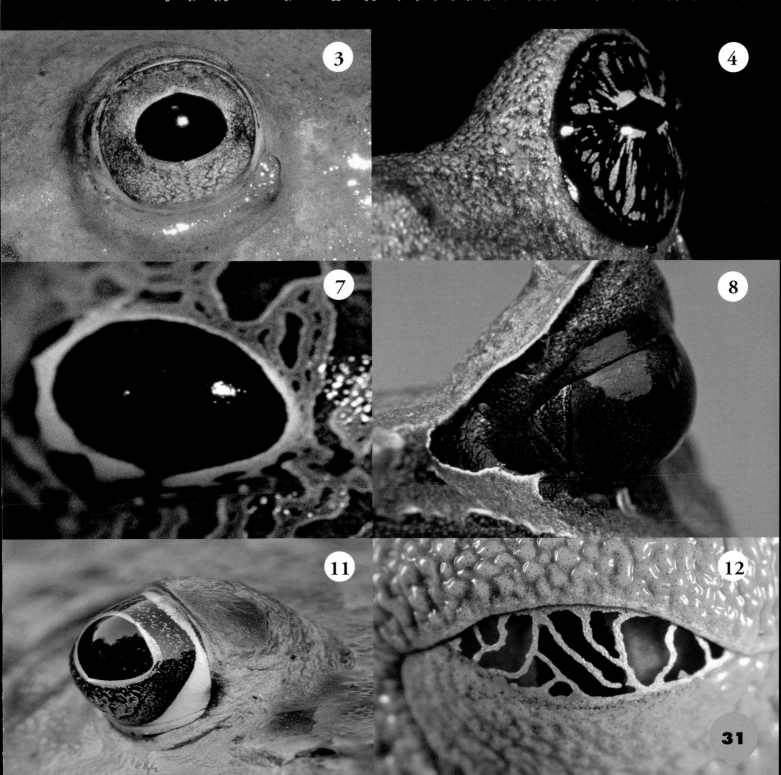

Answer: the fake eye is number 7, which is actually the back of a dwarf frog. Here are the names of the other frogs:
1. Dumeril's bright-eyed frog 2. Common big-headed frog 3. Water-holding frog 4. Poisonous tree frog 5. Smoky jungle
frog 6. Mossy frog 7. Dwarf frog 8. Long-nosed horned frog 9. Red-eyed tree frog 10. Bronze frog 11. American
bullfrog 12. Red-eyed tree frog

31

THE GLASS FROG

With its amazing see-through body, the glass frog blends in perfectly with its surroundings. This little frog hangs on to leaves with tiny, round–ended toes that almost seem to melt into the leaf surface. It lives in Central and South America

3 – 7 cm (1 – 3 in)

MOST GLASS FROGS live high in **THE** *rainforest* **CANOPY.** At such a height, the trees are covered with **clouds** all year round and the **frogs' skin** is kept nice and *moist*. They come down from the canopy to lay eggs.

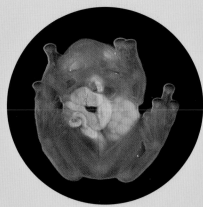

Glass frogs are more transparent from beneath. You can even see their hearts beating busily in their chests.

Glass frogs lay their eggs on leaves that over-hang running water. The male frog stands guard and protects the eggs from parasitic flies.

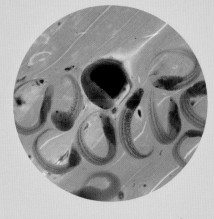

When the tadpoles hatch, they drop down into the water. They have powerful tails and are well-adapted for life in fast-flowing forest streams.

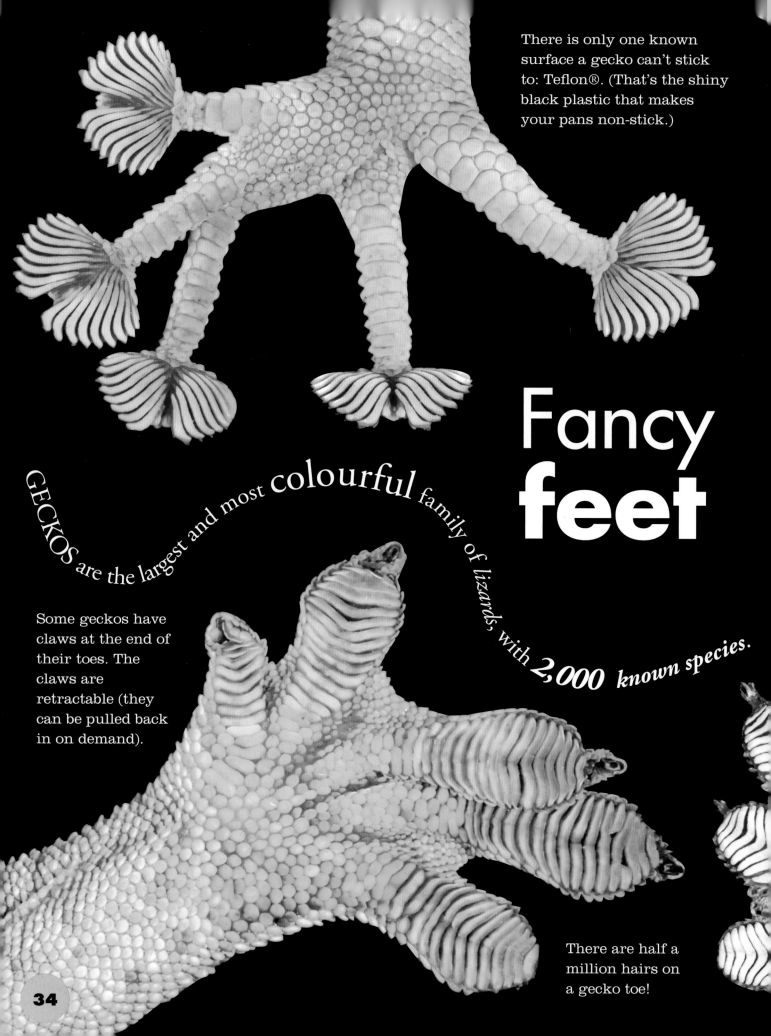

There is only one known surface a gecko can't stick to: Teflon®. (That's the shiny black plastic that makes your pans non-stick.)

Fancy feet

GECKOS are the largest and most colourful family of lizards, with 2,000 known species.

Some geckos have claws at the end of their toes. The claws are retractable (they can be pulled back in on demand).

There are half a million hairs on a gecko toe!

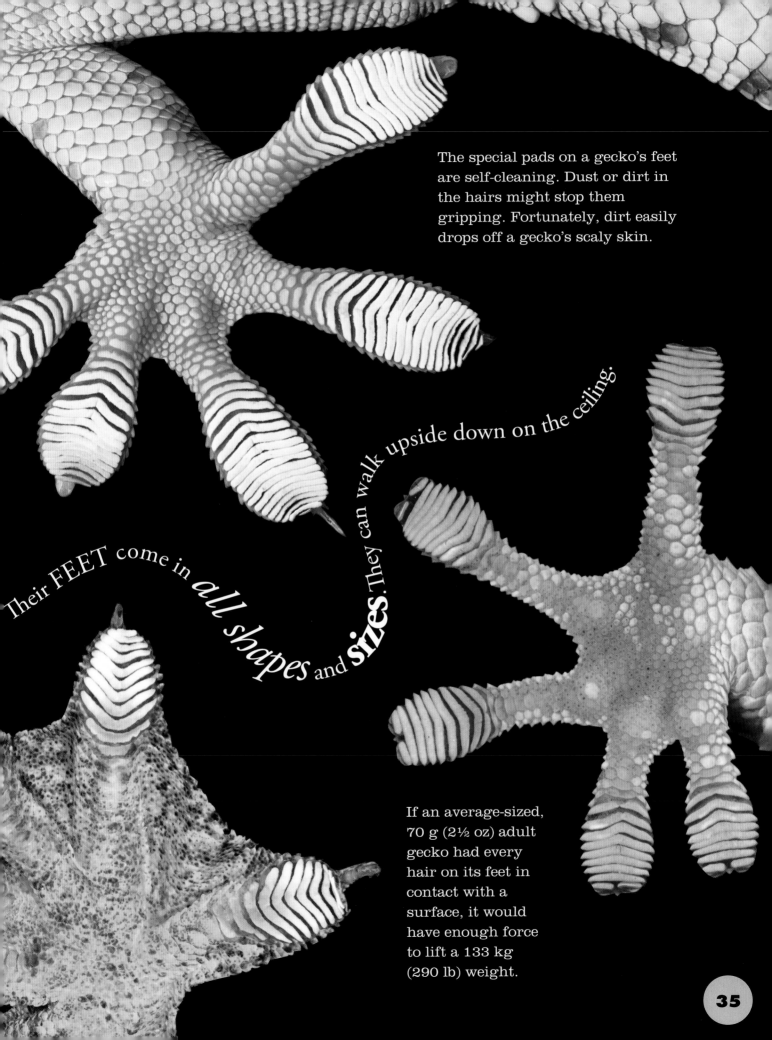

The special pads on a gecko's feet are self-cleaning. Dust or dirt in the hairs might stop them gripping. Fortunately, dirt easily drops off a gecko's scaly skin.

They can walk upside down on the ceiling.

Their FEET come in *all* shapes and **sizes**.

If an average-sized, 70 g (2½ oz) adult gecko had every hair on its feet in contact with a surface, it would have enough force to lift a 133 kg (290 lb) weight.

THE WATER-HOLDING FROG

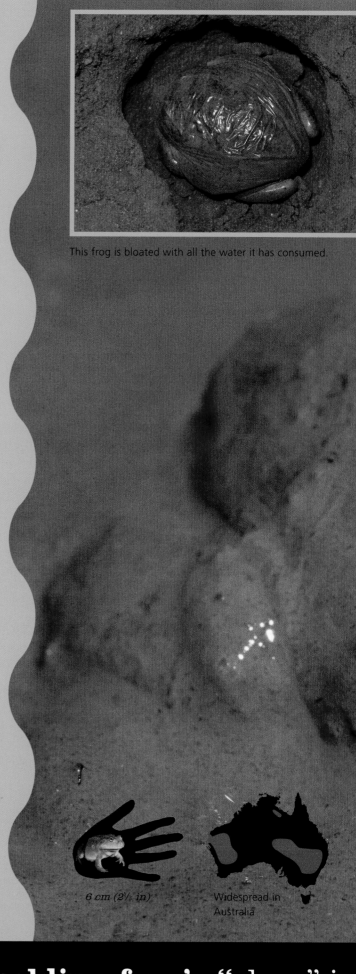

This frog is bloated with all the water it has consumed.

◆ Where does it **LIVE?**

The **water-holding frog** *(Litoria platycephala)* lives in Australia. During the rainy season, the frog absorbs water and in doing so puts on 50 per cent of its own body weight! To avoid losing this water during the dry months, it creates an underground home to stay in. As the mud is still wet from the rainy season, it's able to burrow down more than a metre (3 ft) beneath the surface. It enters a summer hibernation and can stay underground waiting for the next rainy season. When it senses the water from heavy rains, it wakes up and starts to resurface.

◆ **STORING** water

The water-holding frog stores water in its bladder and beneath its skin.

◆ "Living **WELL**"

Aborigines used to dig up the frog to extract drinking water. They used the frog as a "living well". To gain access to the water they squeezed the frog.

◆ **FEEDING** time

When active above the ground, it lives in water bodies. It feeds on other frogs, tadpoles, and small insects.

◆ **EGG** laying

A female usually lays more than 500 eggs in one go! She lays her eggs and then goes into a hibernation. She enters this state in order to prevent damage from extreme dryness and heat.

6 cm (2½ in)

Widespread in Australia

The term for a **water-holding frog's** "sleep" is

efore...

...normal state, a
...er-holding frog is just
...(2⅓ in) in length.

After...

When it has consumed half
its own body weight in
water, its body is enlarged to
12 cm (4 ½ in) in length.

*When active, it
lives in puddles,
pools, and streams.*

TOP 10
DEADLIEST

Most **reptiles** and **amphibians** are perfectly *harmless* to people, but a few can inflict **lethal bites** or *kill* with a touch of their *poisonous skin*. Here are some of the **world's deadliest cold-blooded killers.**

DEADLIEST AMPHIBIAN

Poison dart **FROG**

Phyllobates terribilis of Colombia can kill you if you touch it. Just one of these tiny frogs contains enough poison to paralyse and kill 50 people. The deadly chemical in the frog's skin comes from poisonous plants, which are eaten by ants that are in turn eaten by the frog. Native Americans use the frog to make poison blowpipe darts.

Inland **TAIPAN**

The inland taipan (*Oxyuranus microlepidotus*) of Australia has the deadliest venom of any land-living snake. The venom, injected by a bite, not only poisons nerves but causes the victim's blood to clot, blocking arteries. Before an antidote was developed, there were no known survivors of a taipan bite. Fortunately the taipan is very shy and bites are rare.

Australian brown **SNAKE**
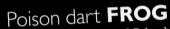

The eastern (or common) brown snake (*Pseudonaja textilis*) of Australia is the world's second most venomous land snake after the Taipan, based on the strength of its venom. Its bite is usually fatal, unless the victim receives an antidote. The venom contains potent nerve toxins, which paralyse the victim's muscles, as well as chemicals that make the blood clot.

Saltwater **CROCODILE**

The saltwater crocodile (*Crocodylus porosus*) of Australia and parts of Asia is the largest reptile on Earth, with big males weighing more than a tonne. Normally seen basking lazily in the sun or wallowing in shallow water, it is capable of explosive bursts of speed when attacking. It drags victims into the water and then rolls around to tear the body apart.

Nile **CROCODILE**

The Nile crocodile (*Crocodylus niloticus*) of Africa kills a large number of people, as locals often collect water or wash in its habitat. It sneaks towards victims with its body hidden in the muddy water and only its eyes above the surface. Then it leaps out and snatches the victim in its jaws before dragging them into the water.

Komodo **DRAGON**

The world's largest lizard, the Komodo dragon (*Varanus komodoensis*) weighs as much as a man and can attack and devour a human being. The lizard kills prey in an especially gruesome way, biting victims with filthy teeth that are covered with disease-causing bacteria. The victim may escape, but the bite turns into a festering wound that can kill.

DEADLIEST LIZARD

Eastern diamondback **RATTLESNAKE**

The bite of North America's deadliest snake can kill in a matter of hours. The eastern diamondback rattlesnake's (*Crotalus adamanteus*) venom contains haemotoxins, which attack the blood and damage a huge area of tissue, potentially leading to loss of a limb or death. Thanks to rapid treatment with antivenom, only a handful of deaths occur each year.

Puff **ADDER**

This bad-tempered African snake is called the puff adder because it hisses and puffs when approached, while curling itself into a tight S-shape, ready to strike. Get too close and it will lunge forwards and sink its long fangs deep into your skin, injecting a venom that attacks the blood. The puff adder (*Bitis arietans*) causes more deaths than any other snake in Africa.

Fer-de-**LANCE**

This South American relative of the rattlesnake preys on rats and other rodents, killing them by injecting venom through its hollow teeth. The fer-de-lance's (*Bothrops atrox*) venom is packed with enzymes that destroy blood cells and body tissues, causing fits of vomiting, diarrhoea, paralysis, and blackouts.

Black **MAMBA**

The bite of the black mamba (*Dendroaspis polylepis*) kills in less than an hour, and without antivenom is almost always fatal. The lethal ingredient in the venom is dendrotoxin, a chemical that paralyses muscles and stops the lungs and heart from working. Death is usually caused by suffocation.

Bamboo pit viper

The heat pit in a python has one section. In a pit viper, it has two sections. The inner one is the temperature of the snake and the outer one heats up when the snake is near to a heat source.

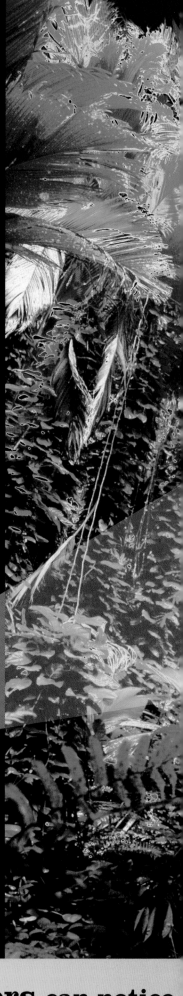

Sixth sense

SNAKES such as pythons, *pit vipers*, and some BOAS are able to PICK UP small *changes* in air temperature around them by using *organs* on their **face**, called heat pits. They detect these changes as *infrared rays* (heat vision). This *sixth* SENSE allows them to locate prey during the night.

This royal python (*Python regius*) sees a thermal image in its brain that allows it to track prey quickly and efficiently.

Royal python

This system is so precise that pit vipers can notice

The FIVE senses

HEARING

Snakes do not have external ears. Their hearing is poor so they rely on vibrations from the ground that pass through skull bones on their lower jaw to their ear. This puff adder (*Bitis arietans*) is sticking close to the ground to sense any vibrations.

SIGHT

Snakes generally don't have great vision, although they are adept at detecting movement. The vine snake *(Ahaetulla nasuta)* is unusual as it has forward-facing eyes that give it binocular vision and a good sense of distance.

TASTE

The Jacobson's organ enables snakes to taste and smell. The organ consists of two sensitive cavities in the roof of the snake's mouth. Their tongue gathers particles that the organ analyzes. Snakes that live in water, such as the green anaconda *(Eunectes murinus)* are able to use their tongue to gather particles underwater.

SMELL

Snakes use their sense of smell to help them locate prey. The common boa constrictor *(Boa constrictor)* detects its prey through scent and taste. Using its Jacobson's organ it is able to work out if prey is nearby. Boas wrap their coils around their victim and squeeze hard to kill them.

TOUCH

From the beginning of a snake's life, it relies on touch for guidance. It uses its tongue and pressure receptors in its skin to touch objects, move, and orientate itself. The Indian python *(Python molurus)* is using its tongue to explore its surroundings.

hanges in **temperature** that are less than a degree.

Gecko FEET

Nothing GOES like a gecko's toes. They even inspire science.

GECKOS are *small lizards* but they've set humans a **BIG** challenge: to **mimic** their *amazing ability* to walk up *WALLS*. Their *secret*? **BILLIONS** of tiny hairs (called *setae*), and long toes to help a lizard grasp the *bumps*.

There's more to a gecko's feet than hair. Their toes bend backwards (compared to ours), and they must "peel" them off a surface a bit at a time. It's like Velcro - it won't slip!

Fan-fingered gecko

The toe-pads on fan-fingered geckos are split into two parts. This gives them extra grip, even compared with other geckos.

There are 14,000 hairs in 1 mm² of a gecko's foot. Each hair has between 100 and 1000 filaments that grip onto the wall as it climbs.

When SCIENCE copies *nature,* it's called **biomimetics.**

STICKYBOT is a **robot** that can **climb SMOOTH SURFACES** such as **glass. HOW?**

Stickybot

Stickybot's feet have rows of stiff, yet bendy "gecko tape" on them. This material produces a sticky force that allows the robot to climb up windows and whiteboards.

STICKYBOT uses **12 motors** to mimic *one animal.*

43

The *newt* that

This captive-bred axolotl looks like an albino – with no pigment present in its skin, but as it has pigment in its eyes it's actually called "leucistic" which means its pigment is reduced.

"Wild-type" axolotls are usually dark.

Wild axolotls are only found in the canal systems of Mexico's Lake Xochimilco. Located close to Mexico City, these canals are threatened by pollution and increased development.

Axolotl means "water-dog" in

ever grows UP

The axolotl is the Peter Pan of the animal world. It doesn't undergo metamorphosis like many other amphibians. Instead, it spends its entire life in a juvenile form, keeping it gills and fins, and living in water. The axolotl grows steadily bigger until it is old enough to reproduce.

Though their numbers are falling in the wild, many axolotls are kept in captivity. Axolotls are popular pets, but they are also studied by scientists because of their interesting life cycles and their powers of regeneration – axolotls can regrow entire limbs. In captivity it is sometimes possible to make the axolotls metamorphose by injecting them with special hormones that trigger growth and development. In their adult form, they look very like their near-relatives, the tiger salamanders.

he ancient language of the Aztecs.

What's for dinner?

The Gila monster stores fat in its thi... stumpy tail. It is th... energy store that allows it to survive... months without f...

Lizards for starters

Most lizards are insect-eaters (insectivores) but some have special diets. Some big lizards are carnivores and eat animals such as birds, rodents, or other lizards. A few lizards are plant-eaters (herbivores).

The binge-eater

The Gila monster (*Heloderma suspectum*) only eats between 5–10 times a year, but when it does, this lizard can consume the equivalent of over half of its body weight. It mainly eats the eggs of birds, or other reptiles.

The insectivore

The Sinai agama (*Pseudotrapelus sinaitus*) is a slender lizard. It has long, thin limbs, which make it good at running over the hot sand when it hunts in the heat of the day. It feeds on ants and other insects, but it also eats sand!

The vegetarian

One plant-eating lizard is the **green iguana** (*Iguana iguana*), which survives on a complex diet of leaves, shoots, flowers, and fruit. It can't digest animal protein well, although it may sometimes accidentally eat small insects and other invertebrates that are attached to vegetation.

The cannibal

The American bullfrog (*Rana catesbeiana*) is the largest of the North American frogs, growing up to 20 cm (8 in) in length. These frogs are voracious eaters and will eat anything they can fit into their exceedingly large mouths. This includes insects and other invertebrates, rodents, birds, snakes, and even other bullfrogs.

Frog food that moves

Most frogs are carnivorous. Nearly all of them eat insects and other invertebrates like worms, spiders, and centipedes, but some of the bigger frogs take on larger prey, such as mice, birds, or other frogs.

The jelly-eater

Leatherback turtles (*Dermochelys coriacea*) are the biggest turtles in the world. They live on a diet of jellyfish and comb-jellies that are mostly made up of water. To get enough energy and nutrients to grow so big, leatherbacks eat the jellies in huge quantities – they sometimes eat their own weight in jellyfish each day.

Sea turtles

The diet of sea turtles varies between species. Some eat a wide range of foods, both plants and animals, but others have special diets, with adaptations that make it easier to eat particular things.

The cruncher

Loggerhead turtles (*Caretta caretta*) mainly eat hard-shelled creatures such as crabs, conchs, and clams. Their big heads and strong jaws help them to crush the shells and they can hold their breath for up to 20 minutes on their dives down to the sea floor.

The fruitivore

Izecksohn's Brazilian tree frog (*Xenohyla truncata*) is one of the very few plant-eating (herbivorous) frogs. Living in bromeliads in the Brazilian coastal moist forest, it eats brightly coloured berries from arum plants and fruit from the cocoa tree. The frog helps to disperse plant seeds in its poo.

The sponge muncher

Hawksbill turtles (*Eretmochelys imbricata*) live around coral reefs, rich in marine life. They can eat a range of prey, but they mainly live on a diet of primitive, plant-like animals called sponges. The turtles are named after their sharp, bird-like beaks that make it easier for them to reach sponges growing in crevices between rocks and corals.

The mite-y eater

Poison dart frogs use poisons in their skin to deter potential predators. They get their poisons from their food. The strawberry poison-dart frog (*Oophaga pumilio*) gets its toxins from a mite that lives in the soil in Central and South America. The frog also eats other small invertebrates. As the frog eats its food, the toxic chemicals build up in its body, which makes it more poisonous.

47

LIVING
FOSSILS

The giant salamanders of China and Japan are the world's largest amphibians. While most salamanders fit in the palm of your hand, giant salamanders grow bigger than your arm – and some longer than the length of your entire body. NOBODY KNOWS how long giant salamanders live for in the wild, but the oldest captive salamander lived for 52 years.

GIANT salamanders have changed *very little* in the last **30 million**

The Chinese giant salamander (*Andrias davidianus*) is the world's largest amphibian, growing up to 1.8 m (6 ft) in length in captivity. It is heavily built, with a flat head and a wide mouth. Like its Japanese cousin, it lives a completely aquatic existence and its short legs cannot support its body weight when it is out of the water.

Chinese giant salamander

Giant salamanders are paler on their undersides.

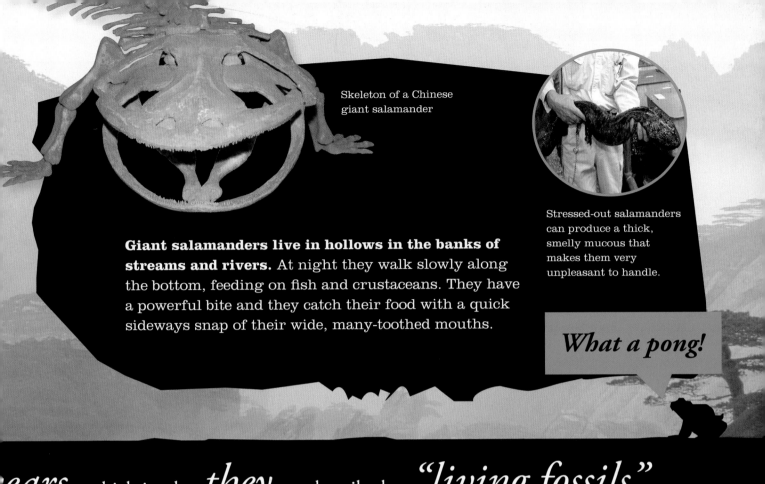

Skeleton of a Chinese giant salamander

Stressed-out salamanders can produce a thick, smelly mucous that makes them very unpleasant to handle.

Giant salamanders live in hollows in the banks of streams and rivers. At night they walk slowly along the bottom, feeding on fish and crustaceans. They have a powerful bite and they catch their food with a quick sideways snap of their wide, many-toothed mouths.

What a pong!

ears, which is why *they* are described as *"living fossils"*.

The Japanese giant salamander (*Andrias japonicus*) is the second-largest amphibian, growing up to 1.5 m (5 ft) in length. The Japanese and Chinese salamanders breathe through their skin. Their skin has folds and wrinkles that increase the surface area, allowing more oxygen in. They like to live in clean, fast-flowing streams but numbers of both species have dropped owing to pollution and dam building.

Japanese giant salamander

Snakes & Ladders

Are you feeling LUCKY? Challenge a friend to a game of **snakes and ladders** and see who gets to the top first. BE CAREFUL not to step on a **snake** – the ones in this game all have *deadly bites!*

You will **need:**
* One or more friends to play with
* A small object to use as a counter for each person
* A dice

How to **play:**
To decide who starts, everyone rolls the dice and the person with the highest number goes first. When it's your turn, roll the dice and move your counter along by the number rolled. If you land on the bottom of a ladder, climb to its top. If you land on the top of snake, slither down to the square at its bottom. If you roll a six, you get to have another roll. The first player to square 100 wins. Good luck!

YOU'VE WON!
100

99

You discovered a new antivenom. Go forwards 5 places.
82

81

79

You mistook a slow worm for a snake. Go back 2 places.
80

61

62

60

59

42

41

40

39

21

22

Coastal taipan

20

19

START HERE
1

2

Hog nose viper

98

97 **96** **95** **94** **93** A spitting cobra spat in your eye. Go back two places. **92** **91**

3

Black tiger snake

87 **Death adder** **89**

84 **85** **86** **88** **72** **90**

75

8 **77** **76** **74** **73** **71**

66 **67** **68** **69** **70**

3 **64** **65**

Beaked sea snake

8 **57** **56** **55** **54** **53** **52** **51**

Death adder **47** You got rattled by a rattlesnake. Go back one place.

8 **44** **45** **46** **48** **49** **50**

33

37 **36** **35** **34** **32** **31**

24 **27** **28** You wrestled an anaconda and won. Go forward 3 places.

Inland taipan **29** **30**

23 **25** **26** **13** **12**

18 **17** **16** **15** **14** **11**

You got squeezed by a boa constrictor. Go back 3 places. **6**

3 **4** **5** **7** **8** **9** **10**

51

Horned lizard

Built like miniature armoured tanks, horned lizards move slowly along the baking ground of their dry desert habitats; stopping to sunbathe, dig burrows, and snack on ants. They have evolved a range of adaptations to help them survive.

13 - 14 cm (5.5 in)

Found in northern Mexico
and south-western USA

Bloody **DEFENCE**

Horned lizards use the spines on their back in self-defence. In addition, they also exhibit a startling form of defence. A network of weakened blood vessels allow them to spray a stream of blood out from their eyes towards attackers. This blood tastes horrible to potential predators.

Dew **DRINK**

Living in dry, desert conditions, horned lizards have evolved to get as much water from their environment as possible. The tiny grooves between the lizard's scales channel moisture from dew that has gathered on its body towards the lizard's mouth, providing a refreshing morning drink.

Body **BEAUTIFUL**

Another adaptation to its desert environment, is the horned lizard's wide, flat body. This allows it to catch rainwater during infrequent desert showers. The lizard raises its tail and channels droplets down to its mouth. Its bumpy, mottled appearance helps it blend into its surroundings and avoid detection by predators flying above.

Sticky **TONGUES**

This ant contain lots of chitin, which is indigestible to a horned lizard. That means the lizard must eat an awful lot of ants to get enough nutrients to survive. Thankfully, the lizard has a secret weapon – a long sticky tongue, which it flicks out like a whip to gather lots of ants.

Horny **HEADS**

The lizards are named for their distinctive horns. These shapes break up the outline of the lizards' heads – making them harder to spot in amongst the rocks and stones of the desert. Their raised brow bumps help to shield their eyes from the strong desert sun, while thick eyelids protect their eyes from stings of their ant prey.

Why did this woman turn people INTO STONE ?

In Greek myths, Medusa was a fearsome, snake-headed monster. Once a beautiful woman, she was transformed by the goddess Athena in punishment for meeting the sea god Poseidon in Athena's temple. In some tales, not only was her hair turned into a twisting mass of hissing snakes, but her teeth became tusks, and her skin was made green and scaly. Anyone who looked at her hideous form turned to stone. Medusa was eventually slain by Perseus, the mortal son of Zeus, the king of the gods. He did not look at Medusa directly, but watched her reflection in his metal shield before beheading her.

Even after she was slain, the head of Medusa still had the power to turn anyone who looked at it into stone. Perseus returned it to the goddess ___ attached it to her shield ___ o scare her enemies.

THE MEDUSA MYTH

WHEN SHE ANGERED THE GODS, MEDUSA WAS TURNED INTO A SNAKE-HEADED MONSTER.

Perseus holding the head of Medusa.

In **search** of the **flappy FROG**

The LAKE TITICACA FROG is the **largest aquatic frog** in the world. The lake it lives in is *3,800* metres (12,500 ft) above sea level, making it a very *COLD* environment to reside in.

Brrr, it's chilly!
The air is thin and freezing cold so the **Lake Titicaca frog** survives by living *permanently* at the lake's bottom. The water here never rises above 10°C (50°F).

The frog doesn't usually need to surface for air as it absorbs oxygen through its skin. It has a lot of skin with plenty of flaps and a big surface area, enabling it to breathe underwater.

The Lake Titicaca frog can measure up to 50 cm (19 ½ in) long and weigh up to 1 kg (2¼ lb).

It does press-ups in order to circulate the water surrounding its body. This keeps its skin folds in contact with oxygenated water.

Lake Titicaca is located on border of Bolivia and Peru.

The Lake Titicaca frog **breeds** in shallow

Why does this frog **exercise?**

waters where it lays about **500** eggs.

Fearsome FRILLS

The frilled lizard (*Chlamydosaurus kingii*) has a loose ruff of skin around its neck. Most of the time it sits flat, like a cape around the lizard's shoulders, but when the lizard is threatened, the ruff expands and the lizard lunges forward, attempting to startle its attacker for just long enough to make its escape.

Tail TRICKERY

Some lizards have developed a startling form of defence, dropping their tails and leaving them wriggling on the ground to distract predators. Skinks, geckos, and slow worms can all detach their tails. Some can grow new tails, but these are never as long as the original.

Clever DISGUISE

The best way to avoid being eaten is not to be noticed. The pygmy leaf-folding frog (*Afrixalus stuhlmanni*) has an unglamorous way to merge in with its surroundings — by looking like a bird dropping. It sits on leaves in full view, and tries to escape attention by sitting very still.

Playing DEAD

Many predators avoid eating animals that are dead, so pretending to be dead can be an excellent way to stay alive. Some snakes stage dramatic mock deaths where they writhe erratically, bite themselves, and fall back to lay still. Sometimes blood trickles from their open mouths.

Toxic to the TOUCH

Some frogs protect themselves from predators by making themselves poisonous to the touch. When this marbled milk frog (*Trachycephalus venulosus*) feels threatened, the poison glands that line its back and neck start to release a milky toxic secretion.

Warning RATTLE

The rattlesnake warns off predators by making an intimidating rattling sound with its tail. Its rattle is made of hollow sections that clash against each other when the snake shakes its tail. The rattles break easily, so the snake adds a new segment to the rattle each time it sheds its skin.

Spitting VENOM

Some cobras spray or spit venom at a threat. The Mozambique spitting cobra (*Naja mossambica*) can target its venom with pinpoint accuracy. This spitting behaviour is so instinctive that young snakes will spit even as they are hatching from their eggs.

Big and SCARY

To convince a predator that it is too big to handle, the black rain frog (*Breviceps fuscus*) puffs itself up to twice its original size. This sudden growth spurt also makes it harder to dig the frog out from its tunnel.

REPTILES and AMPHIBIANS use a variety of ways to **defend** themselves against their enemies. They **spit, rattle, trick,** and **scare** their way to safety.

travel blog

The LEATHERBACK sea turtle loves

Travel **FACTS**

Leatherback sea turtles are big travellers. One leatherback was tracked over an epic voyage of more than 20,000 km (12,425 miles). Leatherbacks travel these long distances to feed their appetite for jellyfish.

User **PROFILE**

Leatherback sea turtle
(*Dermochelys coriacea*)
Leatherbacks are the largest species of sea turtle, and one of the largest reptiles on Earth. An adult leatherback can weigh more than 450 kg (1,000 lb).

Size: 1.2–2.4 m (4–8ft)

Departure time

Adult sea turtles spend their lives in the world 's oceans. They roam large distances in search of food and mates. Adult females also make long excursions to breeding beaches, usually where they were born, to lay their eggs. Experts are still researching how sea turtles find their way back, but they believe sea turtles use Earth's magnetic field, the sea's chemistry, and their memory.

A built-in swimsuit
The leatherback's shell (known as a carapace) is made of a tough leathery cartilage material, which gives the sea turtle its Latin name.

Life's a beach
Once the female leatherhead has found a beach, she digs a small hole in the sand using her back flippers. She then lays about 100 eggs and covers them with sand. Sea turtles usually nest at night when it is safer.

Once a sea turtle hatchling makes it past any beach predators and into the

o travel and swims from warm tropical seas to cold, temperate waters.

new journey

e eggs take about two months to incubate in the sand. The baby sea
rtles, known as hatchlings, can take days to dig their way out.
atchlings normally emerge at night and make the long journey
ross the beach to the lapping waves. This is a dangerous time for a
tchling because they are vulnerable to predators, such as birds and
abs. About 90 per cent of hatchlings never make it to adulthood.

Where to go?
The hatchlings use their
flippers to travel to the sea.
Experts believe they know
the right way to go because
of the light reflected from
the water (even at night)
and the slope of the beach.

Sea turtle **SPECIES**

- Hawksbill
- Green

- Loggerhead
- Olive Ridley

- Kemp's Ridley
- Flatback

ocean, it sets out on a swimming frenzy. It will keep paddling for up to 48 hours.

61

LOST & FOUND

WANTED

The Southern gastric-brooding frog (*Rheobatrachus silus*) has not been seen in the wild since 1981. After mating, the female swallowed her eggs, switching off her digestive system to allow the larvae to develop. After 6–7 weeks, the female regurgitated her young.

WANTED

The golden toad (*Incilius periglenes*) fell prey to climate change, with rising temperatures and erratic rainfall. Fewer breeding pools meant that frogs gathered in greater numbers and this allowed disease to pass quickly through the population.

WANTED

The Darwin's frog (*Rhinoderma darwinii*) has an unusual snout. The male uses his vocal sac to hold the tadpoles until they turn into young frogs. Numbers are declining because the frog's habitat is being destroyed through drought and deforestation.

WANTED

Last seen in 1955, the Hula painted frog (*Discoglossus nigriventer*) was once found along the eastern shore of Israel's Lake Hula. When the Hula marshes were drained in an attempt to reduce the incidence of malaria and make way for agricultural land, it also wiped out the species.

Certain AMPHIBIANS and REPTILES are declining in numbers or being lost altogether. However, lots of **new species** are being *found* every year. Although they can't replace the lost animals that become extinct, they can give scientists hope for the future.

FOUND

In 2009, a survey found that 200 possible new species of frog were living on the island of Madagascar. Statistics like these are *exciting* as they give scientists promise of finding **new populations of other animals**. Earth contains so many surprises – scientists have to be willing to explore remote places to find and identify new species, although every now and then they'll find them in places that have already been explored.

Occasionally, species new to scientists have been known to locals for years. The **bitatawa monitor lizard** (*Varanus bitatawa*) was found by scientists who were walking across a field in the Philippines in 2010. However, the locals had been hunting it for a long time. Scientists missed it because it doesn't come down from the trees very often.

Discovered in Indonesia's Foja Mountains during an expedition in 2008, this little frog has a long, **Pinocchio-like** inflatable nose that expands when the male is calling out. He was seen sitting on a bag of rice in the scientist's campsite and is thought to be one of about 150 species of Australasian tree frogs.

Is it a bird? Is it a plane?

The Wallace's flying frog *(Rhacophorus nigropalmatus)* is also known as the "parachute frog" and is one of the few aerial amphibians. The membranes between its toes and the loose skin on its sides help it to glide through the air, although it doesn't actually fly.

Found in Malaysia and Borneo

10 cm (4 in)

18–20 cm (7–8 in)

South East Asia

I'm a nocturnal creature so I remain still during the day. I rely on my brown skin with bark-like markings to allow me to blend in with the trees. My ability to camouflage myself means I can remain undetected.

I am a Kuhl's flying gecko
(Ptychozoon kuhli) and I love jumping from trees! My strong, webbed feet help me glide through the air. The flaps of skin along my flanks and my flattened, frilly-edged tail also help to control my descent.

Kuhl's flying gecko is a reptile that lives in tropical forests. It's one of several lizards that "fly" through the forest and jump from trees when escaping danger.

When I'm resting on a tree, I often face head-down. This allows me to take off quickly if I need to. I'm always ready to jump and glide.

Don't LOOK UP

The **paradise tree snake** is capable of *gliding among high trees* in tropical forests. It dangles from the end of a branch and decides on its direction of travel. It then *pushes its body* away from the tree, **pulls in its stomach**, and flares out its ribs so that it is twice as flat as normal. It glides through the air in a motion of **lateral undulation** (wave-like movements that propel it forward) in line with the ground so that it can land safely. It can glide distances of up to 100 m (328 ft). It's considered to be the **most adept** of the flying snakes.

Watch out for that snake. It's flying!

The PARADISE TREE SNAKE has a **slender** body and a **long** tail. It can MEASURE up to *0.9 m (3 ft)*.

It's a daytime **hunter** and lives on a *diet* of lizards, frogs, bats, and birds. Its TOXICITY is not dangerous to humans.

How did **frogs'** legs shock SCIENCE?

In 1771, a chance discovery on professor Luigi Galvani's experiment table led, eventually, to the invention of the first battery – without which our lives today would be very different. **So how did one small hop for an amphibian become a giant leap for science?**

In further experiments, Galvani made the legs hop right across the table!

Luigi Galvani was a biologist at the University of Bologna, Italy. He was experimenting with frogs' legs and static electricity when his metal scalpel touched the brass hook that held the legs. Suddenly, the legs twitched!

Volta termed Galvani's discovery **Galvanism.**

Luigi **Galvani**

A **shocking** discovery

Just after Galvani's accidental discovery, it happened again. In a separate experiment, Galvani's assistant touched the frog's sciatic (spinal cord) nerve with his scalpel while he was taking a spark of static electricity from a storage jar. Galvani wrote, "Suddenly all the muscles of its limbs were seen to be so contracted that they seemed to have fallen into tonic convulsions."

Galvani realized that electricity had made the legs twitch, but where did it come from? He mistakenly concluded that the frog's bodily fluids must have been a source of electricity, which he called "animal electricity".

Science owes a lot to Galvani, including the study of bioelectricity (electricity in a body's nervous system) and the process of "galvanizing" (or coating) metal to protect it.

One thing **leads to another**

Galvani published his ideas in 1791, when scientist **Count Alessandro Volta** read them. Convinced that Galvani was wrong, Volta repeated the experiments and found that electricity did not come *from* the frog – but that wet tissue in the legs *allowed electricity to flow* between the metal instruments holding the legs. This gave Volta an idea: a pile of copper and zinc discs with layers of wet card between them would not only conduct electricity, but could also store it. This "Voltaic pile" was the first battery.

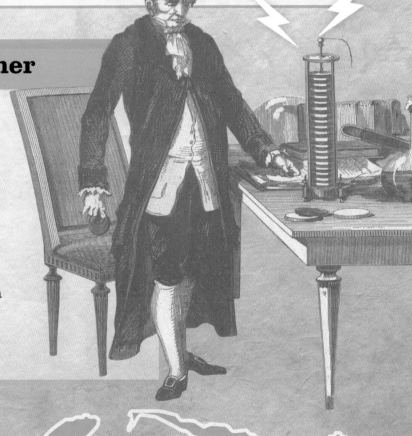

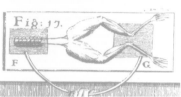

Today, this area of science is electrophysiology.

How to survive an encounter with a crocodile or an alligator

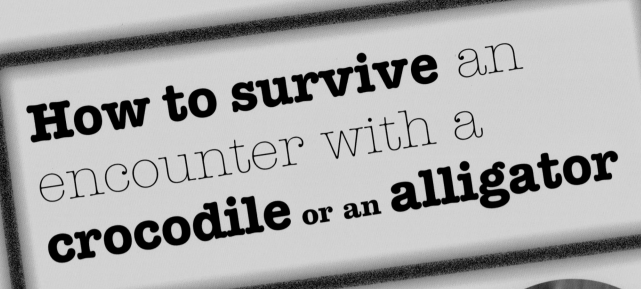

The **jaws** of **CROCODILIANS** are so **strong**

1. Do your research and keep an eye out!

Swim in designated areas only. Alligators and crocodiles tend to hunt at dusk or in the night so avoid swimming at these times. Crocodilians often only show their eyes and nostrils above water so you probably won't spot them easily.

2. Give them space!

You need to avoid going too close to crocodiles and alligators. 4.5 metres (15 feet) is usually enough room to keep between you and them.

3. Catch me if you can!

The average adult can outrun a crocodile or alligator on land. The fastest land speed for a crocodilian is only 17 kph (10 mph).

4. Don't scare them!

Avoid the banks of a river if you're on a boat coming around a bend. Crocodilians like to bask on the banks and will react in self-defence if you scare them. If you spot a crocodile or alligator try to let them know you're there by slapping water with your oars or by blowing a whistle.

5. Get help as soon as you can

If a crocodilian is defending their young or their territory they might bite their opponent quickly and then let go. However, they are more likely to bite their prey and not release them. If you manage to get away from their grip then you should seek medical help quickly.

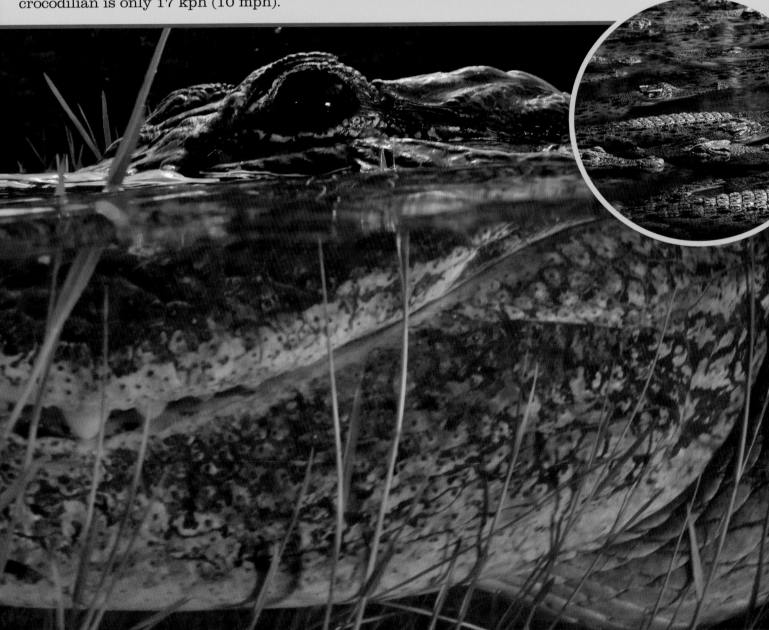

they can **CRUSH** bones when they close!

WORKING WITH
amphibians and reptiles

Animal **KEEPER**
Animal keepers are responsible for looking after animals in zoos or wildlife parks. The amphibian and reptile keepers must be expert herpetologists. They need to know about how these animals live in the wild, what they eat, how much exercise they need, and what temperature and light conditions they need to live in.

Exotic animal **BREEDER**
Reptiles and amphibians are fascinating animals and many people like keeping them as pets. Taking animals from the wild can be bad for wild populations, so specialist breeders supply the pet trade by rearing animals like frogs, snakes, and lizards in captivity.

PHOTOGRAPHER
Successful animal photographers get to travel the world and have to know an awful lot about their subject to track it down and get the perfect photo. It's also not always a comfortable job – carrying heavy equipment in difficult terrain, and camping in remote locations is part of the challenge.

You want to be a what?

A **HERPETOLOGIST**

Zoology is the name given to the *study of animals*. Herpetology is a branch of zoology and is the study of **reptiles and amphibians**. A herpetologist is an expert on these animals.

Veterinary **SURGEON**

Some vets are specially trained to deal with animals such as reptiles and amphibians. They know lots about the health and lifestyles of these creatures and how to care for them in the wild or in captivity. Working with large reptiles can be a hazardous profession as a bite from an alligator is more serious than one from a dog.

Snake **HANDLER**

If you've got a snake problem, who are you going to call? Professional or volunteer snake handlers can be called in to remove snakes from houses and other places where they can come into contact with people. These may be escaped pets or wild snakes living where they shouldn't – looking for shade in the summer months.

Biomedical **RESEARCHER**

Some species of amphibians and reptiles produce toxins and poisons. Biomedical researchers study these chemicals and look at ways in which they can be of use to humans. More than 200 chemicals produced by amphibians and reptiles have been found to be of use in human medicines.

How does this **lizard** walk on **water** ?

The **green basilisk lizard** is often referred to as the "*Jesus Christ lizard*" because it appears to walk on water. How it actually manages this **"miracle"** is by running short distances using its hindlegs. Its toes have fringes of skin that open out to create more surface area.

"These **curious** and strange-looking lizards gain their name from Greek mythology. Made up of parts of a snake, rooster, and lion, the **basilisk** was able to kill a man just from one look. The name basilisk means *"little king"* in Greek, which seems appropriate considering the crests on its head, back, and tail."

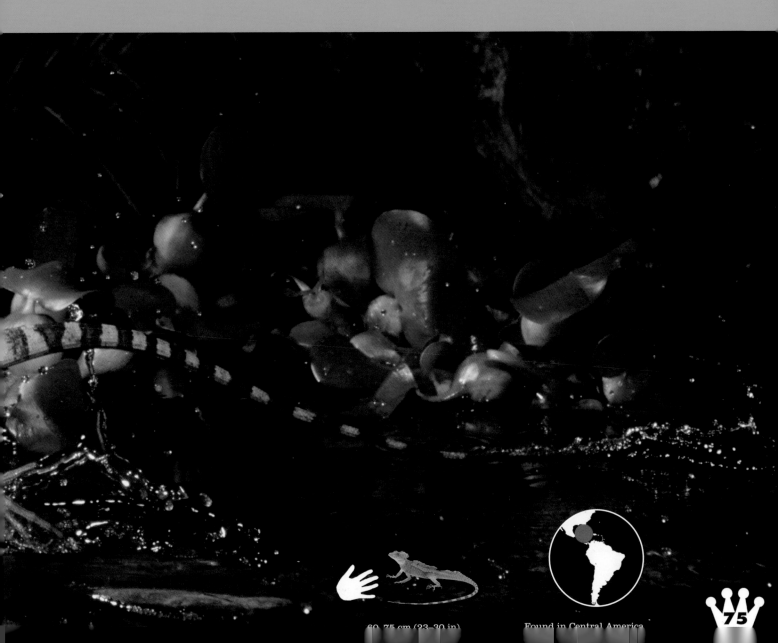

60–75 cm (23–30 in)

Found in Central America

RECORD BREAKERS

Most **POISONOUS**

The Colombian golden poison frog (*Phyllobates terribilis*) is the most poisonous frog, and the most poisonous vertebrate, in the world. It holds enough poison to kill 20 humans or 20,000 mice.

BIGGEST Snake

Asian reticulated python (*Python reticulatus*) which can grow up to 9.6 m (31½ ft) in length. The heaviest snake is the green anaconda, weighing up to 227 kg (550 lbs).

SMALLEST Reptile

This title is shared by two geckos, both measuring only about 1.6 cm (0.6 in) as full-grown adults: the Virgin Gorda least gecko (*Sphaerodactylus parthenopion*) and the dwarf gecko (*Sphaerodactylus ariasae*).

LONGEST FANGS

The Gaboon viper (*Bitis gabonica*) is a venomous snake found in sub-Saharan Africa. The largest of the vipers, it can reach over 2 m (7 ft) in length and has huge fangs, measuring up to 5 cm (2 in) in length.

FASTEST

The black spiny-tailed iguana (*Ctenosaura similis*) can run at a top speed of 35 kph (21¾ mph) – making it the world's fastest reptile. The fastest snake, the black mamba, can move at 19 kph (12 mph).

MOST EYES

Tuataras and many of the lizards have three eyes. The third eye is made up of light sensitive cells just under the skin on the top of the head. This "eye" can detect light and dark but can't make out shapes.

RECORD SPIT

Spitting cobras have a special type of fang with a small hole through which the venom is injected at high pressure. The Mozambique cobra can spray its venom over distances of 2–3 m (5½ – 8¼ ft).

BIGGEST clutch of eggs

Hawksbill turtles (*Eretmochelys imbricata*) can lay over 200 eggs in a single clutch. During the turtles' breeding season, which runs from July to October, female turtles may create 3–5 nests, each with a separate clutch of eggs.

STRANGEST life cycle

One contender for this title has to be Labord's chameleon (*Furcifer labordi*). This reptile spends most of its life (up to 7 months) as an egg, weathering the desert droughts. It lives for only a few months after hatching.

The **LOUDEST**

The couqui frog (*Eletherodactlus*) is a small Puerto Rican tree frog, measuring just 4 cm (1½ in) in length. For something so small, it is incredibly loud, and its distinctive "co-kee" call has been measured at over 100 decibels.

The **MOST TEETH**

American alligators have between 70 and 80 teeth. These are long and pointed teeth, but gradually wear down but are replaced by new teeth. An alligator can go through 2,000 to 3,000 teeth during their lifetime.

The **OLDEST**

The oldest vertebrate (animal with a backbone) is thought to be a Seychelles giant tortoise nicknamed Jonathan. Historians believe that he is now at least 178 years old.

Best **SENSE OF SMELL**

Komodo dragons (*Varanus komodoensis*) will readily feed on rotting meat. They smell with chemical detectors on their tongues and can sense dead animals up to 10 km (6 miles) away. Komodo dragons are the world's largest lizard.

Biggest **LEAPS**

Most frogs can leap over distances of ten times their own body length and some species can jump up to 50 times their body length. The largest frog in the world, the Goliath frog (*Conraua goliath*) can jump almost 3 m (10 ft).

LONGEST TONGUE

Chameleons can have tongues that are as long, or even longer, than their bodies. It takes them less than a second to shoot their tongues out, and the sticky saliva on the tongue's club-like tip traps its insect prey.

MOST DIFFICULT to eat

One contender for this title must be the armadillo girdled lizard (*Cordylus cataphractus*). This lizard is covered in thick and spiky, armour-like scales. It can roll itself up into a ball, making itself even more unappealing to potential predators.

LARGEST REPTILE

The saltwater crocodile (*Crocodylus porosus*) is the world's largest reptile, growing up to more than 7 m (23 ft) in length. Not only the largest, but also the heaviest, saltwater crocodiles can weigh over a tonne.

MOST **POISONOUS** Snake

Sea snakes are the most poisonous snakes in the world. The beaked sea snake (*Enhydrina schistosa*) can produce enough venom in a single bite to kill 50 people.

The Chinese giant salamander.

GLOSSARY

adapt to change, becoming suited to a new place or a new use.

aestivation a kind of deep sleep that animals fall into, sometimes called "summer sleep".

amphisbaenian worm-like, legless reptile found in tropical climates.

animal breeder someone who organizes the birth of baby animals in captivity, and looks after them until they find a new home.

animal keeper someone who looks after animals in a zoo or wildlife park.

antidote a remedy that counteracts the effects of a poison.

antivenom a medicine that treats poisoning from a snake, spider, or insect.

aquatic describes anything growing or living in water.

bask to lie resting in the sunshine.

biomimetics science that copies nature.

captivity when animals are kept confined, and looked after by people.

carnivore an animal that eats meat.

cold-blooded describes animals whose body temperature is controlled by the temperature around them.

coma a state of deep unconsciousness.

crocodilian one of the order of reptiles that includes crocodiles, alligators, caimans, etc.

endangered species animals that are at risk of extinction (no longer existing on Earth).

electrophysiology the study of the electrical properties of living tissues and cells.

evolve to change gradually.

extinct a species that has declined and disappeared entirely from the planet.

eyespot skin marking that looks like the eye of another animal. Eyespots are there to fool predators or prey.

fertilize when male and female cells join together to produce a new life.

fins flat projections on fish or mammals that help them propel or guide their body through water.

gills organs used to breathe under water.

hatch when a new animal breaks out of an egg or pupa.

herbivore an animal that eats plants.

hibernate to go into a deep sleep for long periods.

incubation to keep eggs warm so they develop properly.

insectivore an animal that eats insects.

invertebrate an animal without a backbone.

lateral undulation wave-like body movements that move an animal (such as a snake) along.

life cycle the pattern of changes that occur in each generation of a species.

markings areas of colour on an animal's skin or fur.

mate when male and female animals come together during reproduction.

membrane thin, flexible sheet or layer that covers, lines, or connects animal organs or cells.

metamorphosis major change in an animal's body during its life cycle, as when a tadpole changes into a frog.

nervous system the network of nerve cells in an animal's body.

predator an animal that kills and eats other animals.

prey an animal that is hunted, killed, and eaten by another animal.

retract to draw in or back. Retractable claws can be pulled back into an animal's feet.

scales small, overlapping plates that protect the skin of reptiles or fish.

sixth sense the five senses are hearing, touching, smelling, seeing, and tasting. A "sixth sense" refers to anything in addition to the five senses.

snake handler someone who is familiar with snakes and knows a lot about them.

species a group of living things that can breed together in the wild.

static electricity a still electrical charge as opposed to a current, which moves.

thermal relating to temperature, especially warmth.

toxic poisonous.

transparent clear, see-through.

tropical describes anything that comes from (or is like) the hot region of the Earth near the equator.

vertebra a small bone in the spine, or backbone.

vertebrate an animal with a backbone.

veterinary surgeon (sometimes called a vet) a doctor who is specially trained to look after animals instead of people.

warm-blooded describes animals who can control their body temperature.

INDEX

CREDITS

The publisher would like to thank the following for their kind permission to reproduce their photographs:

(Key: a-above; b-below/bottom; c-centre; f-far; l-left; r-right; t-top)

Alamy Images: 19th era 2 62br; Heather Angel/Natural Visions 48br, 49tl; blickwinkel/McPhoto/PUM 28b; blickwinkel/Woike 18cla; Rick & Nora Bowers 53br; Bernard Castelein/Nature Picture Library 5cr, 16tc, 16br, 29b; Stephen Dalton/Photoshot Holdings Ltd 17tc, 64cr; E.R. Degginger 50br; Jason Edwards/National Geographic Image Collection 19cla; Richard Ellis 3fcra (turtle), 47cra (turtle); Emily Françoise 4cl, 47cla (turtle); Eddie Gerald 46c (sinai agama); Alex Haas/Image Quest Marine 18cl; David Hancock 73cra; Tom Joslyn 62 (background), 63 (background); Thomas Kitchin & Victoria Hurst/First Light 19cra; MaRoDee Photography 18c (frame); MichaelGrantWildlife 41ftr; Michael Patrick O'Neill 41fcr; Mihir Sule/ephotocorp 40t; Stuart Thomson 4tl, 39bl; Kymri Wilt/Danita Delimont 56fbl, 57fbr; Todd Winner 70-71. **Ardea:** Ken Lucas 48b; Pat Morris 49b. **Biomimetics and Dexterous Manipulation Lab Center for Design Research, Stanford (BDML):** 43, 43cra. **CGTextures.com:** 46c (leaves), 46cr (leaves), 46-47t (background), 58-59; Richard 46bl, 46-47c, 47bl, 47fcrb; César Vonc 46cla, 46bc, 47tr, 62cl (paper), 62cr (paper), 62bl (paper), 62br (paper), 63c.
Corbis: Bryan Allen 60-61; Bettmann 55c, 68cr (background); Milena Boniek/PhotoAlto 29clb; Alessandro Della Bella/EPA 27fbr, 76tr (finger); Reinhard Dirscherl/Visuals Unlimited 22-23; DLILLC 42fbl; DLILLC/PunchStock 18cra; Macduff Everton 55 (mosaic); Michael & Patricia Fogden 51fclb; Jack Goldfarb/Design Pics 16tl, 16crb, 17tl, 17c; Clem Haagner/Gallo Images 61bl; Mauricio Handler/National Geographic Society 77br (sea snake); Chris Hellier 76br (chameleon); HO/Reuters 63clb; Wolfgang Kaehler 77tr (tortoise); Jan-Peter Kasper/EPA 44cl, 44-45; Thom Lang 60tl; Wayne Lynch/All Canada Photos 59tr, 60crb; Thomas Marent/Visuals Unlimited 76tl (frog), 77c (frog); Joe McDonald 22cb; Micro Discovery 42bl; Ocean 7ftr, 16clb, 70bl, 80crb; Rod Patterson/Gallo Images 76bl (cobra); Jerome Prevost/TempSport

73bc; Kevin Schafer 77tl (frog); Brian J. Skerry/National Geographic Society 60cl, 60fcrb; Kennan Ward 60cr, 61c; Ron Watts/All Canada Photos 17cb; Jim Zuckerman 16bl. **Dorling Kindersley:** BBC Visual Effects - modelmaker 11br; Mike Linley 3fbl (frog); Natural History Museum, London 3ftl, 11bl, 24c, 24clb, 24cb, 24fclb, 46fcra (african dwarf crocodile egg), 46fcra (indian python egg), 46fcra (nile monitor lizard egg); Oxford University Museum of Natural History 10bl; Jerry Young 3bc (crocodile), 39tl, 46fcra (gila monster), 50-51t, 73tr; David Peart 19cl, 61cr. **Dreamstime.com:** 3drenderings 66bc. **FLPA:** Ingo Arndt/Minden Pictures 61cl; Michael & Patricia Fogden/Minden Pictures 62cr, 62bl; Thomas Marent/Minden Pictures 30bl, 31bl; Colin Marshall 47cr (red barrel sponge); Mark Moffett/Minden Pictures 47fbl; Cyril Ruoso/Minden Pictures 70cr, 77tc (crocodile).
Fotolia: Dark Vectorangel 76-77 (trophy); Jula 76tl, 76tc, 76tr, 76cl, 76c, 76cr, 76bl, 76bc, 76br, 77tl, 77tc, 77tr, 77cl, 77c, 77cr, 77bl, 77bc, 77br. **Getty Images:** Altrendo Nature 70cl; Apic/Hulton Archive 69tl, 69br; Creativ Studio Heinemann 16cb; Digital Vision 59bc; Digital Vision/Michele Westmorland 77cl (komodo dragon); Flickr/Ricardo Montiel 46crb (sparrow); Gallo Images/Dave Hamman 39br; Iconica/Frans Lemmens 25br; The Image Bank/Art Wolfe 2; The Image Bank/Kaz Mori 73cla; The Image Bank/Mike Severns 23tr; National Geographic/George Grall 20-21; National Geographic/Jason Edwards 31cla, 36-37, 71cr; National Geographic/Tim Laman 63crb, 67; National Geographic/Timothy Laman 64l; Photodisc/D-Base 12bl; Photodisc/Lauren Burke 44l, 45r; Photodisc/Nancy Nehring 76c (iguana); Photographer's Choice/Cristian Baitg 12br; Photographer's Choice/Grant Faint 48-49t; Photographer's Choice/Jeff Hunter 47c (yellow sponge); Photographer's Choice RF/Peter Pinnock 61crb; Photonica/David Trood 1clb; Purestock 41fbr; Robert Harding World Imagery/Gavin Hellier 56c (hat); Oli Scarff 72cla; SSPL 68cla, 68c; Stone/Bob Elsdale 12-13, 23tl; Stone/Keren Su 48ca, 49t (background); Taxi/Nacivet 40-41; Heinrich van den Berg 17ca, 80tl; Visuals Unlimited/Joe McDonald 53cr; Ian

Waldie 72cra.
iStockphoto.com: Brandon Alms 64fbr; craftvision 68tr, 68br, 68fcl; kkgas 68cr (ink), 69tr, 69ftr. **Kellar Autumn Photography:** 34-35. **Thomas Marent:** 32-33, 33br. **naturepl.com:** Miles Barton 77bl (lizard); John Cancalosi 53tr; Claudio Contreras 5tr, 47fcr (turtle); Nick Garbutt 18cr; Tim Laman 65tl, 65r; Fabio Liverani 58tr; Tim MacMillan/John Downer Pr 65l, 66tl; George McCarthy 58br; Pete Oxford 21tr, 56bl, 56br, 57t, 57bl, 57br; Premaphotos 58bc; Robert Valentic 36br; Dave Watts 58tc. **NHPA/Photoshot:** A.N.T. Photo Library 36tr, 51cl, 51br, 53crb, 62cl; Anthony Bannister 59br; Stephen Dalton 45cr, 64crb; Franco Banfi 77bc (crocodile); Nick Garbutt 76tc (snake); Daniel Heuclin 26-27, 27tr, 30br, 76cl (snake); David Maitland 31br; Mark O'Shea 51c; Oceans-Image/Franco Banfi 47cr (yellow sponge); Haroldo Palo Jr. 59tc; Gerry Pearce 51tc; Jany Sauvanet 31clb. **Photolibrary:** Olivier Grunewald 61fcl; Joe McDonald 74-75; Oxford Scientific (OSF)/Emanuele Biggi 72bc; Oxford Scientific (OSF)/Michael Fogden 64tr; Peter Arnold Images/Kevin Schafer 18c. **PunchStock:** Stockbyte 18ca (frame), 18clb (frame), 19cra (frame), 19c (frame). **Science Photo Library:** 69cra; Suzanne L. & Joseph T. Collins 17tr; Georgette Douwma 28cl; Dante Fenolio 33tr; Fletcher & Baylis 41fcra; Pascal Goetgheluck 40bl; Alex Kerstitch/Visuals Unlimited 33cr; Edward Kinsman 41cl; Thomas Marent/Visuals Unlimited 30cla, 30clb, 31cra, 31crb; Nature's Images 30crb; Dave Roberts 10c; Sinclair Stammers 30cra; Karl H. Switak 16cr; T-Service 41tl. **Igor Siwanowicz:** 8bl, 42r, 52-53. **Paul Williams/Iron Ammonite:** Arkive 49tr. **Brad Wilson, DVM:** Dr. Luis Coloma 56c (frog).

Jacket images: *Front:* **Corbis:** Nikola Golovanoff c; Sprint cl, cr. *Back:* **Corbis:** DLILLC cl. **Getty Images:** Photonica/David Trood br. *Spine:* **Corbis:** Ocean b. **Getty Images:** Photodisc/Adam Jones t.

All other images © Dorling Kindersley
For further information see:
www.dkimages.com